Where Being Belongs

by

Ayaz Angus Landman

Grosvenor House
Publishing Limited

This book is published by
Grosvenor House Publishing Ltd
Link House
140 The Broadway, Tolworth, Surrey, KT6 7HT.
www.grosvenorhousepublishing.co.uk

This book is a work of fiction. Any resemblance to
people or events, past or present, is purely coincidental.

A CIP record for this book
is available from the British Library

Paperback ISBN 978-1-83615-515-7
eBook ISBN 978-1-83615-516-4

For the children of Gaza

Life, it seems, is a mystery and despite cultural assumptions, we have little idea of who we are, why we are or what it's all about. Our great history is one of emerging from the sea and through millennia of vicissitudes and victories putting a man on the moon, dominating and capitalising as we have gone. So successful have we been, we now face an existential crisis that demands of us a deeper reflection and that we begin to face these questions we have so far mostly avoided.

We have avoided the questions precisely because they can't be answered and our rationale has been either, "what's the point" in asking what can't be answered or we have divested ourselves of them by opting for a higher power that relieves us of the question entirely. Now, both these options are coming under pressure from the evolutionary imperative which demands more.

These prayer poems are my contribution to such an imperative and I hope may engender the love, beauty and truth that is the antidote to a world in crisis.

June 2025

Where Being Belongs

All form suffers
the vicissitudes.
Only a permanent patience
can take me
to the other side of the sky,
and so it is I am always just a half breath,
no more,
from where being belongs.

Broken Hallelujah

Born an ember
A fierce love
Longing for Original Fire
I kindle

The innocent
I tend

In order to abide
I nurture

In order to invite
I constantly remove the ash
Of yesterdays
Broken Hallelujah

Diamonds in our veins

The old well
Still delivers
Sweet water
Lakes lap
On ancient shores
As down the brown river
Runs the current
Of all our yesterdays
Offering us the invitation
Delivering us
Both belonging
And iridescent damsels
Sweeping us
At once
Both gleeful and heartbroken
Into yesterday's tomorrow
Where rewilded
By a blustery sun
We leave
This royal and ancient acre
With more depth of flow
Perhaps
And a hint of what
It might mean
To have diamonds
In our veins.

For all @ The Irish Constellation Camp
June 2023

Manifesting Violets

There is no such thing as mastery
of wind wave or any other thing.
The only thing on offer is communion,
a moment without location,
finding itself empty
so happy, then,
as to manifest
violets.

The Friend's Advice

I ask:
As civilisation teeters
in the smoke and tears
of yesterday's grievance,
what am I to do with my guilt?
"Don't have an opinion"
the Friend replies.
"Just take a moment,
not to secure
an outcome
but to become your own prayer"

The Unexpected

Don't take sides
you have no idea
what's going on here
or even who you are!
Instead,
break bread forever with
all who will come and sit naked
with you,
and always have a spare seat
available for the unexpected.

The Open Road

I love beauty
it takes me out
onto
the open road.
More and more I allow
its flow
realising that in truth
I can possess nothing
as I am
the open road,
along which, down which, over which
all must pass.

Each In our own way

Love alone is what we seek
each in our own way.
A solution to
the Great Cleaving,
a moment we all recall
each in our own way.
Fields empty in winter and bruised skies
give us pause.
Gratitude for grass and birds
and the way light breaks.
How we bring ourselves to healing
by licking the tears of our enemies
children.
Finally the footprints left
that ache
we give to God
each in our own way.

Understanding God

Don't try to understand God
there is no such thing.
Perhaps try to know of that
exquisite place in your being
that longs.
There, hold steady,
don't move
only be moved
and perhaps in time you will find
the question answers
itself.

Understanding Wetness

Poets don't answer questions.
Not satisfied with "seaside"
they want to tumble and tangle
in seaweed
and understand wetness,
not as a consequence of water,
but as its essence.

The Primordial Charge

That which is radiant within
is my flourishing,
my sovereignty.
This is not because of the alignment
of stars but because of
some primordial charge,
that like molten gold within
the mountain,
is deep, pure and inalienable.

Ruin

The grief within the grief
is the last defended place.
Fearful of my shame it makes me
lie about my longing.
Who would have thought
such a small private place
would be the cause of all my agonies
and that unless I bleed out
it will be my ruin?

My Best Lines

I write my best lines
when I can't sleep
because I belong to the night.
Abandoned dreams blow in
like leaves in a gust
through the open door,
or
a pattern of shadows
on the nursery ceiling,
and I'm feeling, sleepy
or contemplative,
or not me at all?

Slaughtering Beauty

Soldiers of the nameless war,
don't miss your chance.
Like a drop falling out of a threatening sky
and landing among the perfectly lustered petals.
Don't miss your chance
to taste the rose water,
the subtle sweet of the immaculate conception,
the unrecoverable moment.
Soldiers of the nameless war
don't miss your chance
as you pass by,
slaughtering beauty
in the name of righteousness.

The Way Light Falls

How can I take credit for this?
Ive just shown up
like everybody else.
Mashed and shaped by experience
the yield is not in my gift.
Perhaps I've opened my mouth
to drink in sunlight a moment longer,
rather than worry about the shade
but that is all,
but its not separate nor mine.
In the end
just the way light falls
among the moving branches.

An Almighty Passion

For the empty page
I do not find words.
At my truest
I am endowed them,
a sequence
begotten
in the mysterious
process,
a pleasure,
like being soothed
by a soft warm wind
blown by an
Almighty passion.

Wild Roses

I love wild roses.
Ashamed of what we touch
I weep.
It seems we cannot bear to watch
beauty climb a wall
without wanting to possess it.
Even in Jerusalem where the shadows are long
we continue to bark at the moon
and shatter the silence of silver
imagining we can possess the gold.
I love wild roses
that climb into the stars and scatter
themselves.
Among them
I find the solitude
And peace of wild things.

The Unbroken Heart

Behind everything defended
Is the unbroken heart.
How painful to watch and feel
the lack.
Who other than You
can we miss in such a way,
and who other than You
can we give it all up for
the instant You ask?

Big Boys Don't Cry

Like a flame denied oxygen
Hubris denies god.
Like
a wasteland strangling itself
lilies remain only as perfumed air
and heartbreak.
Its true
only in tears redemption,
but big boys don't cry.
Big boys don't cry
Big boys don't cry

Ripening

A full flavour ripening
can't be rushed.
Only the seasons
with time spent kicking
cans down alleys
or staring out of the window
at nothing going on.
Only the seasons
can bring through the quality
the taste of a certain
unfathomable patience.
A moment's flash of
Home
where I know
You are waiting
whensoever I might drop in.

Thy Will

I wait now
just a half beat.
The guarded moment
that turns me into a fully
participating witness
like sovereign air,
no longer lost, but
not found.
Like a tension between
two poles,
an invisible current of fire
that sparks out of the seeming
nowhere only
as pure expression of
Thy Will,
my freedom.

The Green Banks

Without shame in her longing
the spring can't wait
to burst the green banks
and sing me back to myself.
In small clumps
and great works
such redemption of
the unspeakably ordinary
makes the poet in me
gasp,
and leave the sodden green page
to the angels.

Clueless

Everywhere we construct,
we build, we try anything.
Desperate
we pull.
Only much later,
perhaps even only when dying,
we push,
Not even…we allow.

Allow,
emptiness to edge into corners
and like the dawn,
allow ourselves to be dreamed
in and out of existence
like a great breath.
Clueless I ask,
am I
the dream, the dreamer or the dreamed?
Clueless
I find myself free,
without a stitch of clothing
on my back.

Emptiness

Everywhere emptiness,
the same emptiness.
Sometimes for a change
I call it 'sky' or even
'love'.
I watch birds fly through
or beauty enjoy its grace,
but in the end I see there
is only one Emptiness
and realise with a smile
centuries old, exactly where
that leaves me.

Leaving

In quiet contemplation
under the watchful eye
of the naked flame,
I become aware,
I don't leave the world
the world leaves me.

Less to lose

Slowly slowly
like a great ice melt
my circle of defeat expands.
With it comes the liberating truth,
the realisation
there is nothing to win,
only less and less to lose.

Better Moments

In my better moments
I who once hoped and longed,
now sit with an empty box
and marvel.

Already Waiting

The true revelation of travel
is not in finding new places
but in the slow realisation
that wherever I go
however wild and untrodden the path
I find myself already
waiting.

Into Emptiness

That which is truly wild
you hardly see.
Like the edges of things
they are shy
and evaporate into emptiness
at the slightest occasion.

Tireless Sovereignty

The sky has no edge
the sun shines equally
but the conquering inadequacy
within
accounts for all the miseries.
Peace lies only in the ice melt,
the clear sweet water,
cold as a bell,
that soothes the fire,
quells the flame
and loves us all
into submission
with its patient tireless
sovereignty.

Fleeting Unassailable Moments

Don't try to get this.
Let the spaces between the words,
the gaps in the language
blow through and shake out.
To be moved is not to
like or dislike.
It comes from somewhere else
and reminds me, in fleeting
unassailable moments,
Of why this is all worthwhile.

Blowing in The Wind

Silence here
possess's me,
not as absence,
but wide armed like the sky.
And what remains
Is still blowing in the wind.

Patiently

The horses
impersonal as the sun
love me to bits,
throwing me in and out of the void,
taking me to the edge.
Patiently,
oh so patiently
teaching me
a way of living that requires
my all.

The Daily Commute

I smoulder here,
barely contained,
wanting to be angry
at the madness,
yet
and yet knowing,
only the wide wilderness
can contain the complexity
and understand what compassion
means here.
For me its just the daily commute
to the Godhead,
to give thanks
and maintain the vigilance
that watches prayer flags
be moved by the tiniest hint of breeze.

This Yield

Don't rush.
Learn to bear the gaze,
nothing but this yield
can ever understand,
the indwelling Christ
of the ordinary moment.

Trudging Moment

There's too much at stake
to keep circling.
Tired trappings
bore me like old stories.
This that I am
is too fine
to be confined,
and yet
only the cloister
offers the discipline of detail,
the commitment to the Gaze
necessary to burst through
this ordinary trudging moment
into Paradise.

Turn and Face

No shining path
for you.
You turn and face.
Battered by the incoming,
like everyone
you become dust
but not the sort of dust
that hides in corners
more the kind that
seeks out sunbeams
in which to dance.

God in you
is never far away
You teach me what it means
to turn and face
and in so doing
you invite me to dance
with you in sunbeams.

(For Sara 30th May 2024)

Wild Poets

Now is the time
and there is only ever now
for wild poets
and the untamed
to put roses between their teeth
and kick high.
Meaning will find the cracks
in us
and dissolve,
leaving nothing
but emptiness
and the rim of salt
where the tide
once lifted us.

(For Steve)

The Yield

Watching darkness effortlessly
yield itself every morning,
or the tide rise and fall
among the rocks,
I know love works like this.
Not so easy as it requires
an inside job,
but once open
finds its place as a
mirror among the stars.

Standing Still

Like a train
moving on either side of me
in the station,
it feels like I'm moving,
but really
I'm just standing still.
Life is like that,
but it just seems not to be.

Shame

In the Garden,
we covered ourselves
and smothered Truth.
Shame is the shadow
behind every cruelty.
Only by reclaiming our being
can we sweeten the air
and stand any chance
of riding the wild horses
out of here.

Gratitude

Naked I am,
and naked I wish to be,
in tears and always kneeling.
Shame has ruined me
so many times
what remains standing is
at my best, true
and when true free
and overwhelmed with gratitude.

Through the Valley

If I sat you still
you would cry,
the ruin of innocence
so close
it brims at your eyelids
at the merest hint of God.
Not the God you don't believe in
of course,
but the one that holds your hand,
moment by moment
as you walk through the Valley.

Pilgrim friend

Pilgrim friend
you know how to hold
The Gaze,
so too do you know
nothing here is safe.
Turned inside out so many times
you have become a patchwork
held together by silken thread
and air.
Faith by now
is not something you have
but who you are,
as for the millionth time
your battered knees bend
for you to kiss the ground
and for your heart to count
its blessings.

(For Randy 4th October 2024)

Pilgrim of Paradise

There is nothing safe here
we leave or are left
by all we hold dear.
Safety can only be found
when shattered and staggering
I am revealed to myself,
not as who I thought I was,
but as a Pilgrim of Paradise
With nowhere left to go.

Where Words Run Out

There is a place
where words run out.
The poetry and music can
only ever take us to the edge.
How close is a matter of genius
but beyond, we travel alone,
surrendered finally
to the celestial mechanics
of a silent Beyond.

Love Prevails

Faith knows only one thing,
that love prevails,
not love as sweetness
but love as truth.
The demolition of form
leaving heartbreak
and joy.
Like the moment
the trapped bird
finds the opening
in the greenhouse roof,
leaving behind only silence
and the memory of a beautiful
being longing to be free.

For Lucia

The Kiss

I have so many jobs,
but only one task...
To return The Kiss
back to You
who gave it to me.

The Moment

Hold it loosely
cradled like a little owl
all feather and grace.
Nature can rage
and be raw.
I am that.
But in the quietude
a certain something
drops slowly.
A practice
always a practice
until the moment comes,
the one I don't want
to miss.

The Broken

Take no position.
Look how beauty steps
out of nowhere
and the blackbird
turns air into song.
All here.
But only available
to the Broken,
those who have given up
trying to know
and instead
are learning how to sing.

Perfect Stillness

Truth is like a
constantly breaking wave
whose restless infinitude
turns everything
to sand,
whilst itself remaining
perfectly still.

Emptiness

This here
is not about
size or quantity.
That is the language of
the dead.
The living know only
of essence,
that which fills
the room with
Emptiness.

Home

What are right and wrong
without direction?
And what is direction
without destination?
We each have our own way
Home.
The horses follow each other,
the wind according to its
mood
and we at our best,
in moments
realise,
we are already
there.

Repay the Ferryman

My life's work
Is to repay the ferryman.
Borrowed at a precarious moment
and leant in absolute faith,
only in acts of kindness can
I return my sweetness
to the soil,
until the day comes
when I find myself all paid up
wandering in wonder down
a dusty road.

Among the Roses

Untangle the knowing.
Be kind.
Learn to enjoy the tiniest
beauty
and gratitude
like a mysterious tide will lift you
speechless among the roses.

A Christmas Carol

Planted deep
in the soil of myself,
I'm seeded to awaken as song.
Beauty touches me,
Truth opens me
and so it is
in moments,
through the impossible darkness
A song of unimaginable tenderness
reminds me of who I am.

Once Wounded

Only once wounded
the cruelties
and all that comes by way
of harm
reminds me.

Once we walked
in the Garden,
so we know what
Communion feels like.

Turn outward and spend
a life chasing down
the hollow dream,
or inward and begin
blade of grass by blessed
blade of grass.
Love has no timeline
but what do you choose,
this moment, this hour, this day?

The Meaning of Love

Form, like lightening
flames the sky
ravishing particles,
brief lives plucked out of the
primordial wonder,
too mysterious to understand
the sweetness of being touched
in such a way,
but graced by such a moment
to learn the meaning of love.

Beyond The Crucifixion

Nothing to be grateful for here
I am that.
That which I long for
I already am.
Compassion, humility, surrender,
joy, love, peace,
the "Be Attitudes",
all come out of the beloved nowhere
Beyond The Crucifixion.

All Being

Theres no such thing as
"any old blade of grass"
Unique and holy
each is an algorithm held in sacred order.
Nothing can be
without all being.

Round Again

Don't fight with me
Or have an opinion
You are not here for that.
You are here to break and
cast yourself on mercy.
Fighting doesn't interest me,
its for those that need
to come around again.

The Second Coming

If the truth is to stand any chance
you have to be interested in
the mystery of soil
and have the patience to
watch apples grow.
You have to feel the sorrow
of the late riser
that misses the handover of the dawn.
But above all, more and more deeply the growing
awareness that that which is without dent,
or at least a modest tear,
has absolutely no chance
Of the Second Coming.

The Spring

Having sat a million years
in the darkness
it flows,
the spring,
to cool my lips.

I don't claim to know
anything anymore
only to give thanks
without ceasing.

Jerusalem Must Yield

Slowly at first
Then all of a sudden
Jerusalem must yield.
The dust is so thick
its almost impossible.
But then as if from nowhere
comes The Moment.
None of us are bystanders
and its only when we lose
connection with prayer
that we take sides.

Holy Site

The dusty feet gather
In the narrowing streets
Turning turning
In a murmuration of longing.
But faith
unlike belief
is not so obvious.
There with the pigeons,
among the hot rafters
The Holy of Holies
is never where we imagine.
The master cares not at all
for rule or ritual.
Only kindness
the sort of kindness
that surprises the eye
with an unexpected tear.

Broken and Holy

This that I am
I already am
and can never not be.
Pursuing the all that glitters
leads to one end
and so a new beginning,
and every moment
is just that.
A broken and holy
Hallelujah.

The Most Holy

In the desert
the wind works
with heat and dust
to bring down the most holy.
Its visitors
must be careful when taking
'selfies'.
Luckily the steepest drops
are well fenced
and guards are on hand
to blow whistles
and restrain those who
lean too far out into the void.

Say "I am"

There is no shame in the silence,
not in the first butterfly
or all that blossoms.
No.
The shame is all ours,
the ticket price we might say
for this ride of a lifetime.
If you want to extract the juice
and say "I am"
show up for The Crucifixion.
If not let other people tell
you how to live.

Imagine

About This
that requires All
I am silence.
Imagine.
A divine intensity,
like springtime in
England.
An invisible indiscriminate
Might
whose passion greens
winter shadows
and sweetens the grass.
Like that
Within
Imagine.

No One is Watching

Refine the prayer
no one is watching.
Only She Who Cares
lines up moments for us
like gold stepping stones.
Everywhere the ordinary
is transfigured
if we can but hold steady
we find that understanding
comes from within,
and so it is we find ourselves
free to return to
a simple life.

The Sky Within

I carry the sky within me.
So it is
I cannot get a fix
on identity.

No matter,
no one can really.
A temporary name will do
surrounded by love
the sky can bless
til its heart's content,
and in so doing
make this a life
worth living.

Internal Dawn

The children don't understand yet
that which you can't explain.
At some point,
The Knowing comes,
like an internal dawn,
heralded by birdsong
and a quality of light
only found at the beginning of things.

Humility

Humility arises
When I find within myself
A purpose beyond myself.

The Pendant Moon

Without the pendant moon
and the skylark,
I would have no explanation
for the sky,
no way of numbering light years,
or even giving myself
a name.
Drenched in mystery
that almost passes me by,
I realise the purpose of love
as emptiness coming to know itself.
I could write about this forever
Or just leave at this
For now.

The Importance of Soil

Avoiding the question,
I live,
trying not to step on the cracks.
Maintaining momentum
my hands remain clean,
but until I understand
the importance of soil
I will never understand
that from which the spring
arises.

Unimaginable Tenderness

That in me which is unbroken
is unreachable.
So it is I circle my sorrow
endlessly.
There is nothing to be done
but bear witness,
until the moment comes when
sooner or later,
restless truth,
relentless as sea on salt
and sand,
will blow through,
leaving nothing but a husk
infused with an unimaginable
tenderness.

Easter Day

I don't need to understand
or be understood.
Into the quiet
the bell rings,
the great forest sighs and
the horses follow each other,
grazing calmly.
Somewhere in the world
Christ is resurrected.
I don't need to understand.
Its just how it is,
just how it is.

Sufi Friends

If you want to live fully
pray without ceasing
and find out what that means.
The half life is not interested
in gods,
but in distraction.
When the knowing comes,
like the dawn rising out of
the seeming nowhere,
prayer and prostration are the only things
of any meaning,
and so beloveds
you will be prepared.

A Permanent Patience

Central to all that turns
Is a permanent patience
Sooner or later it will deliver up
An internal yield to
The indwelling Christ
and with it a joy that is
the end of all longing.